Remarkable Customer Service... and Disservice

Case Studies and Discussions to Increase Your Customers' Delight

Rebecca L. Morgan, CSP, CMC

Remarkable Customer Service ... and Disservice: Case Studies and Discussions to Increase Your Customers' Delight

Printed in the United States of America.

ISBN eBook: 978-1-930039-50-6

printed book: 978-1-930039-28-5

How to order:

Quantity copies may be ordered directly from www.RebeccaMorgan.com.

Visit us online for updates and additional articles.

This book is dedicated to all the unsung customer service heros, past, present and future.

And to my clients who have allowed me to witness their exemplars in action, and to help create more customer service stars.

Books by Rebecca Morgan

Books

- ▲ *Calming Upset Customers*

- ▲ *Grow Your Key Talent: Thought-Provoking Essays for Business Owners, Executives and Managers on Developing Star Staff*

- ▲ *Inspiring Others to Win*

- ▲ *Life's Lessons: Insights and Information for a Richer Life*

- ▲ *Professional Selling: Practical Secrets for Successful Sales*

- ▲ *Remarkable Customer Service ... and Disservice: Case Studies and Discussions to Increase Your Customers' Delight*

- ▲ *TurboTime: Maximizing Your Results Through Technology*

MP3s

- ▲ *Making Time Work For You*

- ▲ *Recipe for Customer Service Success*

All can be ordered at www.RebeccaMorgan.com

Contents

Help Your Staff Shine

Managers scratch their heads when observing their staff, wondering, "What makes some employees exemplars of customer service, and some far below par?" While motivated — and de-motivated — employees often act on their own, it's their manager who either encourages great service — or doesn't. If the manager rewards those who go out of their way to serve customers, others will see that's the level of service expected. And if a manager either lets someone slide or doesn't pay attention, others will see how little they can do.

Whether your customers are internal or external, there is always room for improvement. Even the most luxurious hotel in the world, the Burj al Arab in Dubai, requires their staff to go through rigorous training each year. Their behaviors are monitored by their managers and each is coached on how they can become even better.

What are you doing to ensure all of your staff is improving? Are you having discussions — not lectures — about customer service at each staff meeting? If not, try it.

How frequently do you listen in on customer conversations, either in person or silent phone monitoring? People want to do their best and if they have the opportunity to get some well-delivered, just-in-time coaching or kudos, they'll do much better.

Key here is "well delivered." No one likes to be lambasted for not doing a job the way their boss would like. Get better at delivering feedback by taking a class or reading a book on the subject. Or ask for feedback from someone you admire and take notes on how they deliver it. Ask for their coaching on how you can best coach your staff.

This book is designed to help you improve your organization's customer service. Through the use of real-life case studies of both exemplary and poor customer service, your team can discuss the lessons and how to apply them to your service delivery.

You can use this book for:

▲ **Improving team behaviors.** Make sure each team member has his/her own copy. Discuss specific case studies in a staff meeting. Solicit ideas on how your organization and/or each team member can utilize the lessons. Ask staff to commit to improve one behavior as a result of the case study.

▲ **Refining your management practices.** Decide how you can integrate each case study's lessons into your organization's processes.

▲ **Enhance specific team member's behaviors.** Meet 1-on-1 to discuss specific case studies that parallel the person's challenges. It's often easier to spot when someone else is performing below par, but not recognize it oneself.

We welcome your ideas, suggestions and case studies for future volumes.

About the Author

Morgan Seminar Group is an internationally recognized consulting, training and development firm, based in San José, CA. Founded by Rebecca L. Morgan in 1980, Morgan Seminar Group partners with clients to create innovative, long-lasting professional development solutions. Our focus is strategic customer service, and increasing people-productivity by providing the right skills for the right people in the right way.

Many recognizable organizations have engaged Rebecca to develop creative solutions to their situations. These include: Apple Computer, Singapore Airlines, Wells Fargo Bank, New York Life Insurance, Microsoft, ING, Hewlett-Packard, Adobe, Applied Materials, Quantum, Seagate, Sun Microsystems, Lockheed Martin, Sony, and Stanford University, among many, many more.

Rebecca L. Morgan, Founder and Principal

Morgan Seminar Group founder and principal, Rebecca Morgan, is one of America's most respected and sought-after customer service experts, professional development consultants, authors and speakers. Her media appearances include 60 Minutes, The Oprah Winfrey Show, National Public Radio's Market Place, *USA Today, Wall Street Journal, San José Mercury News,* Malaysia's *Star* newspaper, Singapore's *Straight Times* and the San Francisco Chronicle. Her ideas are so solid, last year Microsoft hired her as their workplace effectiveness spokesperson.

Rebecca's books, recordings, videos and learning tools exemplify the excellence she creates in all of her work. She's authored four popular books — two have been translated into nine languages. Additionally, she's co-authored four others; one is a fund-raiser for the US Olympic team. Her books include: *Calming Upset Customers, TurboTime: Maximizing Your Results Through Technology, Professional Selling: Practical Secrets for Successful Sales,* and *Life's Lessons: Insights and Information for a Richer Life.*

One of an Elite Few Professionals

Rebecca is committed to continuous learning and growing, especially since that is what she imparts to others. She has demonstrated this striving by receiving the Certified Speaking Professional (CSP) designation conferred by the National Speakers Association (NSA). At the time, the ten-year-old designation had been earned by only 215 people in the world—less than seven percent of the 3700 members of NSA.

The CSP is a designation of achievement earned through proven speaking experience. It is awarded to individuals who have completed a comprehensive application process and met NSA's stringent criteria.

She has also earned the professional designation Certified Management Consultant (CMC) from the Institute of Management Consultants (IMC). She is the fifteenth professional in the world to earn both the CSP and the CMC designations.

Candidates for the CMC undergo a thorough investigation of their consulting experience. They are interviewed by a panel of senior consultants to verify their competence. Additionally, candidates must pass a written examination demonstrating their knowledge of the IMC's Code of Ethics.

Case Studies and Discussions of Exemplary Service

What's Your Definition of Above-and-Beyond Service?

My friend, internationally acclaimed concierge-level service speaker Holly Stiel and I were talking about what constituted world-class service. I had just returned from Malaysia and Singapore where I stayed in 4- and 5-star hotels. I gave her a few examples of what I thought was extraordinary service:

▲ The bellman who took me to my room of the 600-room at the Berjaya Times Square Hotel called me by name two days later, with no contact in between." That's standard at a high-end hotel," Holly said.

▲ The concierge at The Legend Hotel who escorted me from the lobby down nine floors to hail me a cab, even though there was a doorman who could do it. Holly shared, "All concierges would assist you in getting a cab if they didn't have another guest waiting."

▲ The front desk clerk at the Gallery Hotel who took my carry-on luggage and escorted me to my room. "All guests should be escorted to their room," Holly said. True, but it's usually by a bellman, not the front desk staff.

▲ The front-desk and bell staff at the Gallery called me by name throughout my week-long stay. "Hotel staff should know and use guests' names all through their stay."

I argued that even though these things might be in the Standard Operating Procedures, they were hardly standard in my experience, or at least not prevalently.

So if these things were supposedly standard at any good hotel, what constitues higher level service at any operation, whether in retail, hospitality, or a call center? What behaviors make up concierge level service? And how could we teach these behaviors, ensure they were being used consistently, and measure the results of their use?

Holly said we had to teach staff how to think like a concierge. She says, "The practice of exercising creativity, ingenuity and efficiency to fulfill a customer request are job requirements that are nurtured and honed by the people who are known in hospitality for ultimate service. The attitudes and skills that make a successful concierge are applicable to many service-oriented jobs, from administrative assistant to security guard, ticket-counter clerk to telephone service representative. It is the spirit in which the job is performed that makes the difference."

But how does one teach resourcefulness? Creative thinking? Putting yourself in the customer's shoes? How do you know when your people are going above and beyond? And what does above-and-beyond look like to your customers? They may think it is just what is expected when you think your staff has bent over backwards to provide a special service.

Holly is the author of *Ultimate Service, The Complete Handbook to the World of the Concierge* — if you want to order a copy, you can do so at www.ThankYouVeryMuchInc.com/.

Adapt the Lessons To Your Situation

1. What are examples of your receiving above-and-beyond service?

2. When have you gone above-and-beyond for your customers?

3. How could you go above-and-beyond more frequently to wow your customers?

Exemplary Customer Service Starts at the Top

I recently learned about two leaders who exemplify outstanding corporate customer service leadership. They are in an industry not known for innovation — automobile sales and service. Rita and Rick Case now own 14 dealerships in 3 states with nearly 1000 employees and own the largest Honda dealership in the world.

How do they do it? As you would guess, they not only hire great people, but they treat them well. The employees in turn treat the customers well. But the leaders have designed ways to reward the customers for continuing to do business with them. Here are a few examples:

- ▲ Rewards program — Customers earn points for every purchase they make. These points can be redeemed for discounts on future purchases, including new vehicles.

- ▲ Free car wash — With a purchase of a vehicle, you get a card that allows you to get a free car wash anytime you want.

▲ Gas station on site — Rewards program members save 5-25 cents/gallon.

▲ Free rental car with service.

▲ Clerk of the Courts office — At their main dealership people can pay their speeding tickets, get their driver's licenses renewed, and get a marriage license. They even have a chapel so couples can get married! Forty to 50 couples a month say their nuptials there.

▲ Salespeople call customers monthly — They tell them how many rewards points they've accumulated, how they can be redeemed, and any specials the dealership is running.

▲ Rick and Rita also show their customers they care about their community by being active on charity boards and chairing large fund raisers. Their main dealership is a voting site. Additionally, after being concerned about people being trapped in submerged vehicles, they manufactured and distributed 50,000 emergency escape hammers.

What could you try that is out of the norm to show your customers you care?

Adapt the Lessons To Your Situation

1. Rick and Rita thought of unusual ways to serve their customers. What do you currently do to serve your customers that is different than your competitors?

2. How can you come up with unusal ways to serve your customers?

3. What can you adapt from this story to implement in your organization?

How does a 7-star hotel hire and train staff to ensure service literally fit for kings?

Service Secrets from the World's Most Luxurious Hotel

W hat makes a hotel 7-star? How do they hire and train staff to ensure service literally fit for kings? Dubai's world-famous Burj Al Arab hotel holds the answers.

Our guide, the gracious and delightful Jonathan Evans, Manager of Learning and Development, took participants from my 4-day "Customer Complaint Management" course on a private tour of the grand hotel. He explained what we wanted to know — how do you hire, train and manage over 1000 employees, including 140 butlers, to deliver best-in-class service to such discerning guests.

To set the scene, imagine sighting the Burj Al Arab (meaning "Tower of the Arabs") in the distance as we approach. It looms off shore 1053 feet high. The shape is representative of the sail on an Arab dhow (boat) which has plied the Arabian Gulf for hundreds (thousands?) of years.

As we get nearer, we see the wall facing shore is white fabric. At night, lights illuminate it with an ever-changing display of solid colors, turning to the next color every 3 seconds. After passing security, we cross the curved bridge to the man-made island on which the Burj Al Arab sits. We pull into the reception circle, passing the Rolls Royces the hotel uses to shuttle guests to and from the airport, as well as to other venues owned by the parent company, Jumeirah.

We are greeted by beautiful men and women offering us dates on a silver tray, cool towels to freshen up, and Arabian coffee. Before us stands a 3-story fountain of dancing water sprays illuminated by different colored lights. We look up at the 590-foot atrium — the Statue of Liberty could fit inside. But we notice something is missing — a Reception Desk. Guests are greeted at the front door by their own personal butler who escorts them directly their room to check in.

There are luxurious couches nearby on which guest are resting. A 30-foot red curved couch invites us to rest while we wait for our escort.

Jonathan greets us and explains that the basis for their exemplary service is their philosophy. All colleagues operate with the companies guiding principles — they call them the 3 Hallmarks:

▲ Smile/greet the guest first. A guest should never have to connect first.

▲ Never say "no" as the first response to a guest. Sometimes you must tell a guest you can't accommodate their request, but that should never be your first response.

⚠ Treat colleagues with respect. It starts from even the term they use — "colleague" not staff, employees or associates. In watching them interact with each other during our tour, they showed courtesy and respect to each other, similar to how they treated the guests.

Jonathan weaves his tale of impeccable service standards as he shows us through the hotel. We pause in the bar after touring the underwater restaurant, Al Mahara, and ask, "How do you hire world-class employees?" Jonathan explains, "We hire for attitude — the rest can be trained." Of course, there are certain jobs that require first-rate attitude coupled with high-skill levels. We asked how they determine attitude in the interview and he said interviewees are given scenarios and asked how they would respond. They also role play some situations. And the applicants are asked how they've handled situations in past.

We are taken to one of the two-story suites to get a sense of the guest's experience. The rooms are lavishly appointed with no detail left unattended. A desk is outfitted with everything you'd need to get a little work done — including a laptop! The living and dining rooms are spacious. The kitchen has a door to the outside so the butler can set up your room service meal or handle any party needs easily without coming through the front door. Of course, each room has a floor-to-ceiling view of the water. And the master bedroom is up a curved staircase. The bathroom is complete with full sized toiletries, including perfume/cologne, body lotions, etc., which guests are encouraged to take home.

Here we get some insight into the colleagues' training program. Each colleague is given a week's orientation upon hiring. Many of them then shadow an experienced employee for a month before being allowed to be on their own. They are required to have 6 hours of training per month, which can include cross training in other departments, or specialized training in their area. So if a waiter had a background in accounting and wanted to explore being transferred there, it is possible to do. Or if he wanted more specialized training in wine to possibly become a sommelier, that is possible.

We take the elevator to the Assawan Spa & Health Club on the 18th floor. There is a beautiful lounge, and to either side two facilities — one for women only and one for mixed genders. In each are pools, work out rooms, massage areas, jacuzzis, showers, etc. They are designed based on ancient Arabian baths. The pool butts up to the floor to ceiling windows overlooking the Gulf.

In the lounge, Jonathan explains the reward system. They have several programs, including Colleague of the Month, Colleague of the Year, and an Exceptional Colleague Award. Additionally, they have an instant reward system whereby managers can give a reward to any colleague s/he has witness going above and beyond.

Next he takes us to the top of the structure — the Al Muntaha restaurant, which juts out from the top of the building 650 above the Arabian Gulf. Here we discuss how employees are trained to handle complaints. Surprisingly, nothing really earth shattering here — it's mostly about active listening.

We take the glass elevator down to the ground floor where we sit outside in the dusk discussing the Burj Al Arab's amazing attention to detail. We learn that each guest has a detailed profile so when they return everything will be just right. This could include their restaurant preferences, room service choices, to how they like their clothing packed or unpacked by their butler. All are kept on file and reviewed before arrival so their stay will be as seamless as possible.

The outside of the structure is cleaned regularly so guests won't see any dirt or sand piling from the ever-present breezes. They even engage a falcon for pigeon patrol, so guests won't have to worry about any unwelcome addition to their head or clothing during their jaunts on the grounds.

Our tour ends at the front door, where Jonathan has thoughtfully provided us goodie bags with a few souvenirs of the property. We have had a glimpse into a world-class organization that few can share.

Adapt the Lessons To Your Situation

1. What can you modify from the Burj al Arab's practices to fit your organization?

Management Makes Right Decision

My friend and I had looked forward to this catch-up lunch. The restaurant was busy even though it was only 11:30.

Upon sitting down, I informed our server I wanted to buy one of their special "free pizza with gift card" deals. I gave her my credit card and she said she'd be right back while we looked over the menu. She returned with my credit card saying there was a problem validating the gift card so she'd try it again after she put in our orders.

We placed our order and continued chatting. Ten minutes later the server appeared saying they were still having trouble validating the gift card. My friend informed her she had to leave in about 45 minutes so was hoping our orders would be out soon. The server was cheerful and said no problem. Another ten minutes passed and still no meals. We flagged down the server and she said the computer froze when they tried to validate the gift card so our orders may have been lost. She asked what we wanted again.

She came back with the free pizza certificate and said

they were giving up on my gift card. We asked about our meals and she said she'd check. They arrived about 10 minutes before my friend had to leave. She could only finish about half, so she asked for a take home box and our bill which we'd like to split between our two credit cards. The server apologized and returned quickly with the box and the check. My friend was now getting anxious as she needed to leave any minute.

The server returned with our two credit card slips. My friend began to sign and discovered both were run on the same card — mine! I told her to leave and I'd take care of it. She did. But the slips were already totaled with no room for a tip. I dug in my purse for enough cash for her tip.

I gathered my belongings and stopped at the reception desk to speak to the manager. I said, "I know you've had computer problems today, but I thought you should know your server put both halves of our bill on the same card and there's no room to add a tip." She said, "That's my fault. I ran them. I tell you what — you had a lot of patience with our screw ups, so how about lunch on us?" And she ripped up both credit card slips.

She did the right thing. Our server was friendly and tried to be of service, but the computer hamstrung her. Yes, she could have checked on our order earlier to discover it had been lost in the system. But there were a lot of problems with our lunch.

Adapt the Lessons To Your Situation

1. What did the service provider(s) do well?

2. What could the service provider(s) have done better?

3. What would your colleagues had done given similar circumstances?

When I wheel in my 30+ year-old 10 speed, they never laugh or make me feel like an old lady riding an antique.

Bike Shop Spins Customer Loyalty

The guys at Willow Glen Bicycles in San José keep knocking my socks off with their service.

Dick and his crew are the kindest, most generous and knowledgeable bike staff around. I've watched them take care of the most proficient cyclist with thousand-dollar bikes to kids on Schwinns. When I wheel in my 30+ year-old 10 speed, they never laugh or make me feel like an old lady riding an antique. I've been to other local bike shops, including the previous owners at this location, and never been treated so well.

Today is a great example. Last week I took in my bike because the odometer/speedometer I bought from them a few months ago was not working. At that time one of the senior techs suggested I get a new battery and he wrote down the battery number. I bought a new battery, installed it and it still didn't work, so today I rode in to see if I hadn't done something right. They tested the battery — it was fine. So Dick, the owner, replaced the unit with a higher level one saying the one I had was defective. He activated it and I was on my way. He wouldn't take anything for the new one as he said he'd send in the old one and get a replacement from the manufacturer.

I asked if I could buy a tire valve cap and he said, "No." I knew he was kidding and he added, "We don't charge for those."

A month ago I brought in my bike to buy some new accessories. I asked the tech if he could also do a few adjustments, for which I was happy to pay. He said, "No problem," did all the adjustments, installed my accessories and I only paid for the merchandise, even though I insisted I wanted to pay for his time. I was told, "No charge."

The last time I took my bike in for a tune up, I was quoted a reasonable standard tune-up fee. When I picked up my bike a few days later, the bill was about half of what I was quoted. I said the bill was wrong as the fee should have been higher. They said I didn't need all the things a normal tune up included so they only charged me for what it needed!

They continually adjust my derailleur, fill my tires to the right pressure, and install accessories for free. They are a delight. When I wait for service I try to find accessories to buy to make sure they are around a long, long time.

Adapt the Lessons To Your Situation

1. What did Dick and his crew do well?

2. How could you adapt what Dick and his team do to engender loyalty among your customers?

She wasn't just doing her duty by perfunctorily inter-acting pleasantly with each person, she seemed actually interested in their responses.

The Paschalis Factor

A s I boarded the flight, I was greeted by a flight attendant. In the course of a year, I'm greeted by dozens of flight attendants, most of whom are pleasant and professional. This one, however, struck me as different.

She not only said "Hello," looked me in the eye, and smiled, she added "how are you today?" in a way that seemed she was really interested in my response, not just a throw away pleasantry. "I'm doing great" I responded. "I'm glad to hear it," she continued, "we're going to have a great flight."

I noticed she interacted similarly with every passenger with whom she came in contact. She wasn't just doing her duty by perfunctorily interacting pleasantly with each person, she seemed actually interested in their responses.

A passenger had difficulty putting his too-large carry on in the overhead bin. She approached him "What do you have in here? Your life's belongings?" She tried to help him stuff it in, but no amount of shoving would get it to fit. "Darlin'" (she's from Louisiana), "I'm afraid this baby just isn't going to make it. Let me just have those strong baggage handlers gently put this in our underbelly." He complied easily.

I chatted with her about her attitude and approach to her work. She was in her late twenties, had been flying for a while, and really liked what she did. "I like people," she stated clearly. "It's clear you do," I confirmed, "but what about difficult passengers?" "I've not met someone I couldn't get through to. I just treat them with respect and don't let them ruffle my feathers. They all come around sooner or later."

American Airlines flight attendant Paschalis Cowell has a special way about her that makes you feel better to have been on her flight. When you find her, tell her I said "hello."

Adapt the Lessons
To Your Situation

1. What did Paschalis do well?

2. What can you adapt from this story to implement in your organization?

She takes the term "customer service" to new heights.

Customer Service Star: Carmel Windows

armel Windows—what's that? Microsoft's newest version of their operating system? A Halloween prank? Is it a window store in that quaint town of Carmel-by-the-Sea? What is it?

Carmel Windows is a customer service rep extraordinaire. Carmel works for my publisher. Every time I interact with her, she takes the term "customer service" to new heights.

For example, when I leave a book order on her voice mail, she not only calls to confirm the order, but tells me when it will be shipped. Then she calls to tell me that it's been shipped and when it's slated to arrive. Sometimes the order is for just a few books.

What makes Carmel go way beyond "good" service? She says she likes the feeling she gets when she surprises people by going beyond what they expect. She says that every order is important because, although someone may be ordering just a few books today, that could lead to hundreds next week.

She told me of a woman who called to order the book *Overcoming Anxiety* because she was apprehensive about an interview the next week. Searching the database, Carmel saw that the book was on back order and wouldn't be available for two weeks. After hanging up, she searched the warehouse for a copy. No luck. Returning to her desk, she found a copy on her own bookshelf. She sent it to the woman with a note saying she knew how important this was, so she sent her own copy.

Now that's customer service!

Adapt the Lessons To Your Situation

1. What did Carmel do well?

2. What can you adapt from this story to implement in your organization?

I didn't see any employee ignoring a passenger, nor acting inappropriately. The only criticism I had was one for management.

Soaring Customer Service

My seminar was for 90 cabin crew of Singapore Airlines. I'd flown from SFO to Singapore, as well as to and from India, on Singapore Airlines, so had scrutinized the staff and their service. I had plenty of examples to sprinkle in my presentation on "Calming Upset Customers."

The good news was nearly all my examples were positive. I didn't see any employee ignoring a passenger, nor acting inappropriately. The only criticism I had was one for management.

Here it is: There was a long line to check bags for my flight home. Only one person was on duty at 6 a.m. for those who checked in online. So while they told passengers to be at the airport 3 hours before departure, which I was, they didn't schedule staff to accommodate those who took their instructions seriously. At 7:00 another employee was added, but by then most of us had waited in line a long time. The queue for those who needed more than to check bags was twice as long, even though more employees were on duty.

What did Singapore Airlines do right?

▲ At SFO the gate agent had to weigh passengers large carry-on bag to ensure it didn't go over the 7 kg limit. He went from person to person in the waiting area with a scale. I watched him get into protracted discussions with people who did not want to check their overweight luggage. He was always polite but firm. Even if someone got upset, he didn't lose his cool.

▲ On board, the stewards and stewardesses (that's what they call them) were not only impeccably dressed and groomed, they were unflappably gracious. In my seminar, I learned that passengers treat them poorly if there is a problem with the individual entertainment system, or if a passenger doesn't like the food. I can't imagine giving a flight attendant a hard time about these things, but apparently lots of people do. The stewardesses were always chipper and happy to fill any request they could. Quite a contrast to some of the American carriers' flight attendants who act like they're doing you a favor to serve you half a can of soda.

▲ Arriving at the Mumbai airport hours before take off, we were uncertain which was our gate, as it wasn't posted. My travel companions and I camped out near a gate we were told was for our flight. About an hour before departure, with still no signage at the gate, a Singapore Airlines gate agent stopped by and asked where we were headed. When we told him, he said we were in the right place and when boarding would begin. This is the first time I've ever experienced an airline employee proactively seeking to be helpful to those in the waiting area.

⚠ In Singapore flying home, I had absentmindedly put a small pocket knife and cuticle scissors in my carry on. Security personnel detected them and put them in an envelope which they put in the checked baggage bin. I was told to give my receipt to the Singapore Airlines personnel in the SFO baggage claim area to retrieve them. Sure enough, there were personnel at the baggage carousel. I gave a staff person my receipt and moments later my items arrived. In the past I've had TSA confiscate these items never to be seen again.

Is Singapore Airlines perfect? Of course not. However, as a frequent flyer I can spot when someone seems to like their job or not. Interestingly, I learned that Singapore Air does not pay its staff top wages. In fact, those attending my seminar came on their day off and bought my *Calming Upset Customers* book with their own money, not the company's. This shows me that the airline knows how to hire people who have an attitude of investing in their professional development, not an entitlement mentality.

If you get a chance, fly on this airline. And report to me about your experience.

Adapt the Lessons
To Your Situation

1. What did the service providers do well?

2. What can you adapt from this story to implement in your organization?

Amara Hotel Exemplifies Superior Service

S ome hotels claim to have superb service. Others actually provide it. Here's an example of some of the outstanding service I received on my recent stay at the Amara Singapore.

Arriving at 6:00 a.m. from my overseas flight, I was informed I needed to check back at 10:00 to see if a room was available for early check in. Or I could pay for an additional night's stay. I choose to cool my heels until 10, and asked where I could change clothes. Expecting to be directed toward the ladies room, I was pleased to be told I could take a shower, use the workout facilities and change clothes in the gym. After stowing my luggage, I set out for the gym.

Stuffing my purse in a locker, I locked it with a self-determined combination, then took a shower. There was only one other woman in the locker room at this early hour. When I came out, I couldn't get in my locker — the code I used didn't work. I asked if she knew where there was a nearby house phone so I could get someone to open it. She said, "I'll take care of it." She pulled out her cell phone and called Security. Within minutes, a man arrived with the master key.

While we waited for Security to arrive, she introduced herself as Margaret Tan, Executive Housekeeper. It's nice to have friends in high places! I asked where I could get wifi in the hotel while I waited for 10:00 to see if a room opened up. She said, "I'll take care of that." She called the Front Desk to arrange a very early check in for me — at no extra charge!

When I later arrived back in my room after doing an errand, there was a small fruit basket and floral arrangement with a nice note from Margaret welcoming me to the hotel. To show my appreciation, I autographed a copy of Calming Upset Customers and sent it to her with a bellman. Later I learned she was so excited, she immediately took it to the General Manager to show him.

On my errand, I bought a gift for a local friend and some wrapping paper. Realizing I had neither tape nor scissors, I stopped at the Concierge desk and asked if I might borrow both to wrap my gift. Tony, the concierge, nearly insisted that I leave it with him for wrapping. I declined as I knew it would just take a few minutes. We chatted as he helped me. He invited me to come to the Club level for a glass of wine during happy hour, even though I was not staying on the Club level.

Outside my seminar room the next day, the Amara training manager bought two copies of Calming Upset

Customers and one of *Professional Selling*. He left his card, so I called him to tell him I'd be happy to autograph them to him. When I was on a break, we met to discuss how I might help them be even better. He asked if I'd meet with the General Manager. Of course!

Suddenly, every staff member seemed to know my name, from bellmen, concierge, front desk, and banquet staff. Many of them introduced themselves after calling me by name and then gave me their card.

The General Manager and I discussed how I might help them improve their performance. During our hour meeting we explored various possibilities.

I know you're asking, would the staff had been so outstanding if Margaret and I hadn't started out so well? I'd stayed at the Amara previously and the staff was great. But I think being a minor celebrity helped bring out the very best in them. So if you go to the Amara, try telling them you're my friend and see what happens!

Adapt the Lessons To Your Situation

1. What did the Amara staff do well?

2. What can you adapt from this story to implement in your organization?

Do You Trust Your Customers?

In a recent vacation to Lake Placid, NY, I was taken down a winding country road to South Meadow Farm. We entered the small room attached to the barn which displayed a large variety of local food stuffs. We were tempted by shelves of maple syrup (light-, medium-, and dark-amber varieties), homemade jam, maple-based candy and other local goodies.

But what was missing was most striking.

A cashier.

This shop was unstaffed. There was a tin of dollars and credit card slips for you to process your own transaction. You either left what you owed and took any needed change, or completed a credit card slip noting your total. The owner came by several times a day to harvest her payments, and I'm told she has only once had anything stolen in many years of operation. She purposely leaves less than $50 in the can so it is less tempting to would-be scofflaws.

In my business, colleagues have shared they will

put a stack of books in the back of their seminar room with a sign for purchasers to deposit $20 in the basket if they want a book. They report rarely, if ever, having books disappear sans payment. I've tried this myself and it seems to work.

Do you trust your customers? Would you allow them to self-service pay if they could? You may say, "I sell to businesses. It involves invoices, etc. We couldn't do anything like that." Think again.

My client Granite Rock took trust to a new level. Their accounting and sales people used to spend a lot of time negotiating with clients who felt they should get a discount if the goods were not what they expected. They started a policy that if a customer felt s/he deserved a discount for goods not up to exceptions, they could send in what they felt they owed with an explanation of why they were taking the discount. Granite Rock rarely pushed back, and they receive invaluable information on how to improve their goods/services. They spent no time negotiating with unhappy customers. Their unhappy customers count was reduced to nearly zero.

Adapt the Lessons To Your Situation

1. How does your organization show your customers you trust them?

2. What else can you do to show your customers you trust them?

Even monopolies can still exhibit excellent service

Even Utilities Can Excel at Service

had a most delightful experience with my water company which shows even monopolies can still exhibit excellent service. But it didn't start out that way.

A few months ago I had a water bill that was four times normal. I immediately called the water company and within a week they sent two seasoned workers to isolate the problem. After 30 minutes of poking around my front yard, they determined I had a broken irrigation pipe.

I promptly called my landscape contractor, and he came over within a week. He discovered it was not a broken pipe, but a valve had been left on, watering my yard 24/7 for over a month. Ugh!

The water company sent me a follow up saying I could apply for a "courtesy refund." I did. I was called and told I didn't qualify. I can understand that as it was completely my fault, since my yard man turned the valve.

A few weeks later I got another call from a different person at the water company. She asked me to elaborate what was on my refund application. She was chagrined that her two veteran employees had misdiagnosed the problem, resulting in another week's leakage. She thought the solution was so simple, these workers should have figured it out within a few minutes. Their failure to do so resulted in my continuing to have the leak, and a higher bill.

She decided to refund me for the month's higher water bill!

Wow!

I hadn't really expected anything since the valve was not the water company's fault.

I appreciated the customer service rep's diligence and compassion. I didn't beg or plead with her, I just gave her the facts. And she went beyond my expectations.

Now that's excellent service!

Adapt the Lessons To Your Situation

1. What did the service rep do well?

2. What could the veteran field employees have done better?

3. What can you adapt from this story to implement in your organization?

I'm always interested in what makes one business success-ful while another languishes.

Great Lessons from a "Burger Joint"

The line of hungry patrons waited patiently to place their order. The newly opened neighborhood burger establishment, Mojo Burger, had already created a buzz by their quality food and their top-notch service. But it wasn't just that they served Meyer Natural Angus beef and fresh, not frozen, fries.

I'm always interested in what makes one business successful while another languishes. There are plenty of fast food places in our community, some independently owned. But this two-store chain has stood out, so much so that I wind up there every few weeks for a quick bite.

So what makes this place stand out, other than their food?

▲ Peter Favre, the owner, surfs each table pausing to ask each person how their meal is, while looking each diner in the eye and waiting for the response. You know he is "the man" as his name tag says simply, "Mr. Mojo." Their web site explains, "After completing the management program at McDonald's Hamburger University, Peter was an instant success with the fast food giant, as he was able to come into any location and improve their volume almost immediately. How? By giving people the finest, most attentive and professional service they had ever experienced. Soon Peter was opening new McDonald's and saving existing ones with his endearing personality and incredible work ethic."

▲ If Peter isn't around, "Mrs. Mojo," his wife Carole, mirrors his behavior. When was the last time you ate at a fast food place — in fact nearly any place — and had the owner or manager come by and make sure your dining experience was good? I've had this every once in a while, but not regularly. And often when they do stop, it seems perfunctory and their attention is fleeting and on to the next table. But not so with Carole and Peter. Each takes a few moments to focus fully on you.

▲ Their staff is friendly and "present." No matter who you interact with from cashier to grill cook, they look you in the eye, smile, and are not distracted by other things. Peter says, "We teach them to think." He adds, "When a customer comes in, I train my employees to act like that customer is their mother-in-law that they're meeting for the first time." Everything — the presentation, the cleanliness, the attention to detail — had better be perfect if you ever want to impress the toughest critic of all.

Mojo's philosophy is, "If it's not right, we'll fix it" and they do. Burger underdone? No problem, we'll redo it. Not enough sauce on your BBQ sandwich? Let us know and we'll add more. The tiniest detail is not too small if it makes a customer happy.

How can you use the Mojo example in your own organization? At the risk of stating the obvious:

- ⚠ **Get in your customers' face — positively.** How often do you call or see your customers and ask for honest feedback? If you aren't having regular conversations with your customers, something is wrong.

- ⚠ **Don't just give lip service.** You have to walk the talk. If you tell your staff to listen to your customers and you aren't, there's a disconnect. They will learn by your example much more than your harping and not being an exemplar.

- ⚠ **Hire and train the right people.** Peter and Carole consider their employees part of their family and treat them that way. If someone isn't a good fit, they move them on. Do you have people around you who you are proud to represent you to your customers? If not, coach them, and if there's no improvement, release them to a company that is a better fit for them.

- ⚠ **Fix what's wrong — now!** Do you fix what your customers' complain about instantly? Or do you hide behind "That's not our job," or "That other department just won't do it right." You can't afford to make excuses. Figure out how to satisfy your customers, even if it's not your department's fault for the problem.

Mojo's web site says, "Mojo Burger's customer return rate is unprecedented. 'We have a very high customer return ratio. How do we do this? With great people, systems, and procedures that produce consistently high-quality, great tasting food in a nice environment for a good value.'"

Amen.

Adapt the Lessons To Your Situation

1. What does Mojo's do well that you can adapt to your organization?

I complimented her on her impeccable attention to the guests and asked what motivated her to treat everyone with such care.

Do Your Staff Focus on Serving Each Customer Uniquely?

She stood at the entrance in her crisp uniform, greeting every arrival. The guests filed past into the hotel meeting room for the local radio and TV broadcasters annual awards banquets. She looked each person in the eye as they passed and said, "I hope you have a great time tonight."

I watched her, noting this out-of-the-norm behavior, even for 5-star hotels, which this was not. After we were seated, she visited each of her tables and asked if there was anything we needed. She chatted with those who wanted to chat and moved silently to pour wine for those otherwise engaged.

I complimented her on her impeccable attention to the guests and asked what motivated her to treat everyone with such care. She said she'd been working in hospitality for over 40 years and loved her job. But the next thing she said stood out for me.

"These people have given me so much joy every day, I'm thrilled to be able to help them make their special night memorable."

This server had a clear vision of who her customers were that evening and how she could give each something from her heart.

Did she do this with every group? What about those to whom she had no personal connection? I didn't think to ask her, but now I'm guessing she found something to celebrate about each group.

Do your employees find ways to relate to each of their customers? Do they think about how to make each interaction special? Do you notice exemplars and compliment them? Or better yet, reward them?

Adapt the Lessons
To Your Situation

1. What did the service provider do well?

2. What can you adapt from this story to implement in your organization?

I was treated to anther example of Singapore Airlines above-and-beyond service.

Singapore Airlines Again Shows Stellar Service

I expected the brief 1-hour flight from Penang, Malaysia to Singapore to be uneventful. Instead I was treated to anther example of Singapore Airlines (SQ) above-and-beyond service.

The flight was reasonably empty, so I took the opportunity to ask the lead steward how he liked the new uniforms SQ had just rolled out. Instead of different colored suit jackets to denote the stewards' rank, they all now wore dark blue suits and their ties were color-coded to their status.

He was affable, as are most SQ cabin crew. He explained how the stewards' ties now coordinated with the stewardess' (their name for flight attendants) dresses. His tie was green, which meant he was a lead steward, and the lead stewardess's dress had a green background.

He good-naturedly asked how I liked the suits. I said the stewards always looked sharp. He said, "What about the tie?" I smiled, saying it looked classy. Seeing that I was playful, he then asked, "And what about my hair?" We both laughed as I said I liked his short-cropped curly hair.

Which then began a laugh-infused conversation about how he didn't like his curly hair, and I shared how my hair, too, was naturally wavy and I often straightened it. We schmoozed for a few minutes.

He disappeared, then reappeared calling me by name. He must have looked me up on the passenger roster. He asked if he could get me anything else, and I jokingly said, "Chocolate?" knowing these short flights didn't often have treats like that, and rarely in coach.

A few minutes later he and a stewardess appeared with a plate of four chocolate cookies on a silver platter. When I delightedly asked if they got them from First Class, they said yes. So he purloined a treat from another class just to make me happy!

We joked and laughed the rest of the flight. I gave him my card and he said he would buy my book *Calming Upset Customers*.

Soon the steward manager came by and introduced himself. He asked about my book and my philosophy on customer service and if I was available to speak to groups. Of course I am!

This was just another example of how SQ turned an everyday encounter into a memorable experience. Even if he hadn't produced chocolate, the interaction with the steward would have made my day.

Adapt the Lessons
To Your Situation

1. What did the steward do well?

2. What can you adapt from this story to implement in your organization?

*I'd begun to see why this is
such a highly rated hotel.*

Outstanding Service at Brunei's Empire Hotel

My 7-night stay at Brunei's fabulous Empire Hotel began at the lobby door. The Manager on Duty greeted me by name as I entered the exquisite lobby. Quite a feat for a 450-room hotel.

At the front desk I was informed I'd have free Internet via DSL. "No wireless?" I asked. The clerk paused, then said, "Hold on a minute." She made a quick phone call and came back with, "I've arranged to have a wireless router put in your room." "Is there a charge for that?" "No charge."

I'd begun to see why this is such a highly rated hotel.

Each of the 10 guest-room buildings has it's own manager and conceirge. The manager greeted me at the building door and took me to my room. She said the router would be arriving shortly — I was impressed that the front desk must have called and informed her. In my room I noticed there was no clock, something I've found commonly absent from SE Asian rooms. I asked if they might have one in housekeeping. She called and was told they did not. She said if it was important, she'd send someone to town to buy one for the room!

On the third day of my stay, she greeted me as I entered the building. She asked if I'd like a room with a better view than the partially obstructed third floor view I had overlooking the South China Sea. I love views, but was also tired from my long days and didn't relish packing and moving. I asked if I could see the room first. She whisked me to the 6th floor with a room overlooking the breakers on the beach, which I love to hear. I said I would like to change, but was too tired to pack tonight so we could do it in the morning. She offered to come pack my belongings and move me!

Adapt the Lessons To Your Situation

1. What did the staff do well?

2. What can you adapt from this story to implement in your organization?

I'd been putting off buying an iPhone for several reasons, but a key one was the horror stories I'd heard about the AT&T customer service.

Fabulous Service From AT&T

I'd been putting off buying an iPhone for several reasons, but a key one was the horror stories I'd heard about the AT&T customer service. I was a happy Verizon customer, often being amazed at the great customer service when I called in with a question.

My Verizon contract had ended. I waited a few more months to see if the iPhone would be available with other carriers after the initial 2-year monopoly. It didn't. I could wait no longer. I pre-ordered mine on June 8, the first day orders could be placed.

I received a notice on June 12 that my number would be ported over to AT&T on the 19th, when I was slated to receive my iPhone. However, the number they were confirming would be transferred was my office number, not my cell phone number. This would not do.

On June 15 I called the AT&T number I was given and was connected to the amazingly helpful Linda (unfortunately I didn't catch her last name). She quickly understood the issue and tried to change the order on her end. She could not without my order number, which I didn't have with me. So she asked if I'd like her to call

Apple to get my order number. She conferenced me in on the conversation with the Apple rep, who was also very helpful. Linda got the needed information, we hung up with the Apple rep and Linda proceeded on her end.

She ran into a snag and said we needed to call Verizon to release the number on June 19. Would I like her to call Verizon? Absolutely! Again, she conferenced me in while she explained to the helpful Verizon rep what we needed. They were friendly and cheerful with each other and with me.

After almost an hour on the phone, she said she'd done everything she could on her end, but that the SIM card would come with my office number on it, which won't work. She said I'd need to go into the AT&T store to get a new SIM card.

I was grateful that she had stayed on the phone and interfaced with the other reps. Others might have just told me to call Apple and Verizon myself and get back to them with the information. Her staying on the line smoothed the process.

I dreaded going into the AT&T store on June 19, as I was sure it would be swamped. I called the store on the 18th to see if there was an expedited line for transactions such as mine, since I didn't need to go through all the paperwork needed as I'd completed mine online and would have iPhone in hand. They said there was no such line, but they expected the lines to die down after 3:00.

I arrived at 3:45 and there was one man ahead of me on the sign in sheet. But the customers with reps seemed to be taking forever. After about 20 minutes, Jeremy, one of the reps, called my name and asked what I needed. He was on hold for something else but said he could help with the SIM exchange as that was easy. He was friendly and helpful, even though he said he'd been at the store since 6:30 a.m. to prepare for the onslaught of customers when the doors opened at 7:00.

Unfortunately, it was not as easy as he thought. He called his manager over. They went into the back room to try to resolve the issue with the main AT&T office. They called Verizon, which hadn't released the number yet. He updated me regularly on the status. He thanked me for my patience. I asked him some questions about my new service while he was on hold with Verizon. He was pleasant and cheerful through the whole transaction.

When I left at 5:00 having it all straightened out, I commented that I might not have been as cheerful after 10 hours of helping a slew of customers. He said he'd had plenty of people who were upset that day with things taking longer than he hoped. He was grateful that I had been understanding. I said it was easy to be when he was so helpful.

At one point, I observed the manager going around the store with a pin knife cutting down the balloons decorating the store. I thought, "How odd that he would spend 15 minutes doing this inconsequential task when 10 customers were waiting for help. Wouldn't it been a better to help customers instead of taking down balloons? No one cared if they were taken down or not, so couldn't it wait until after hours or the next day?"

Adapt the Lessons To Your Situation

1. Do your service providers help the customer get their issues resolved so they can use your product, as Linda did?

2. Are your folks cheerful and helpful, even after 10 hours on their feet on a very busy day?

3. Are your managers doing unimportant tasks while customers wait in a long line?

Apple's unique take on tech support

Tech support has been the bane of many companies. Watching their costs skyrocket, many began charging for tech support beyond a limited time frame. Many (most?) tried outsourcing to India and the Philippines, but some have pulled back to US-based support after their customers screamed about unintelligible "help."

My experience with Apple's tech support was no different — until recently. As a Mac user since 1989, I even formed a MacUsers group to help sort out Mac issues, which then morphed into an listserve. Luckily, Macs don't need a lot of tech support, or at least my needs were pretty minimal.

Last week I bought an iPhone. Having difficulty with a few gnarly issues, I went to their online support site to search the knowledgebase. Unable to find the solution, I clicked on the "Online Support" link., then "Speak to an Apple Expert." There, one enters their product serial number, describes the issue and — get this — choose a convenient time for an Apple Expert to call you! I choose "now" and within seconds my phone rang. The very helpful (US-based) tech helped me sort out my issues for 20 minutes.

Wow!

Later on, I had issues understanding how to do what I used to do with my old PDA, so I signed up for an iPhone class at a nearby Apple store. Since I also had some complicated issues with my laptop, I scheduled a "Genius" appointment for right after the class. The Genius Bar is where you get live help on the Apple equipment you bring in, generally at no charge. There is a charge if they can't fix your issue and have to send it out, but I've only rarely been charged, and have been informed of the charge in advance of their proceeding.

The iPhone class as well worth my hour, even though I'd figured out many of the basics on my own. Kent, the Apple sales representative guided the 10 of us in attendance. He had an amazing amount of patience with the broad spectrum of attendees' experience. Some people were at the "how do I turn it on?" phase, and others of us had figured out all but the nuances.

After class, I took my list of issues to my Genius appointment. I luckily got Caley, a very experienced, patient and thorough tech who figured out all of my troubles. Some required reinstalling software, which he did graciously, and while files were loading he answered my questions, even recommending third-party solutions and finding them on the Web so I got the right product number. One fix helped me save $160 in buying new software.

Since my issues were complicated, it took four hours to get it all straightened out. He politely asked if I minded if he helped others while my computer was installing software. Of course, I said yes.

I noticed employees wore three different colored Apple t-shirts. I asked one wearing orange what the T-shirts signified. "The orange t-shirted people are the bosses. We help customers quickly get the right help. The light-blue folks are the sales people. They help people buy the right product for their needs. And the dark-blue wearing ones are the Geniuses. They repair relationships."

Read that again: "They repair relationships." Not "They repair your equipment." Apple understands that if there's something wrong with your computer, iPod or iPhone, there's a problem with their relationship with you. So a Genius's job is to make sure that the problem is fixed. Thus making people happy with their Apple product. This of course, creates absolutely loyal fans. Apple is famous for having the highest loyalty percentage in the computer business, with customers, like me, never even considering buying any other brand.

Adapt the Lessons
To Your Situation

1. What is your organization's take on customer support? Do you make it easy — really easy — for customers to get their problems resolved?

2. Are you calling them to resolve their issue once a problem has been communicated? Are you focused on repairing relationships?

Lightning Source Lightens My Load

ightning Source is a provider of short-run and print-on-demand book publishing for small publishers like me. I'd researched dozens of short-run printers for my latest books, and decided on Lightning Source because of the many benefits they offer and their reasonable prices. Little did I know they'd also set themselves apart by their stellar service.

After an initial hiccup of not hearing back for months from a sales rep, even with my repeated follow ups, I finally got into their system. Publishers upload our books' contents and covers with ease. My questions were always cheerfully answered by my client services representative Joan Williams. I'm sure she must have encountered my basic questions thousands of times, but she never sounded irritated.

But Lightning Source's service blew me away when I needed proofs of my two latest books (Remarkable Customer Service…And Disservice and Grow Your Key Talent) to be sent to me in Brunei. I needed them to show at an HR Summit in Singapore, which was the next stop on my speaking tour. I chose to have them sent to Brunei instead of Singapore as I'd be there for 7 days and thought if UPS missed by a day or two I was most likely to get it there.

Lightning Source's staff went above and beyond for me. Usually it takes a week or so to get a new book into their system and for a proof copy to be generated. I uploaded the documents 10 days before I left for Brunei thinking that would be plenty of time. Unfortunately, I made some mistakes which weren't caught by the Lightning Source staff until a few days later. I had to fix them and reload the documents. The clock was ticking. All the documents were successfully uploaded only the day before I left!

The cost for shipping a proof copy is a standard $30/book. Since I was sure it would be more cost effective for me to have both books sent together in one package, I asked if this could be done. It was not how Lightning Source usually did things — they usually shipped a proof as soon as it is off the press and my books may be printed a few days apart. I was asking for a modification to their SOP, which I know in my own business is often asking for disaster.

I was also sure it would cost way more than that to ship to Brunei via UPS, Lightning Source's shipper. But Joan couldn't determine how much. She tried asking the shipping department, but they couldn't help. I talked to Joan's boss, Leah Charlton, who determined the fee would be the same, even to Brunei. Wow! Really? With such short notice? Yes. She also figured out how to send them together so one didn't take days longer than the other. She coordinated everything, making my life much easier!

The books arrived during my Brunei stay. They looked great. I displayed them and took orders at the HR conference. I couldn't have done it without the fabulous service of Leah, Joan and the other Lightning Source staffers.

Adapt the Lessons To Your Situation

1. Do your people answer the same question they've heard millions of times with patience and pleasantness?

2. Are your people able to accommodate unusual requests with grace?

3. Are they resourceful in finding ways to get what the customer wants without incurring outrageous costs for the customer or your organization?

Sensitive Service From Insurance Company

My father died a few months ago and left us with a maze of assets to sort out. We found two life insurance policies with Prudential so filed the proper paperwork. Within a few days of receipt, Andrea, an amazing helpful claims representative, called all the beneficiaries to say she'd found another policy and would use the same documentation to pay it out, if she could just have our verbal agreement! Wow!

I worked in the insurance industry decades ago and knew the kind of documentation that was usually required, often making people go through what seemed like unnecessary hoops. But Andrea and Prundential didn't make us file an additional documents — which would have been tedious and time consuming since we are spread throughout the country.

Andrea understood that her job was to make our life easier, especially after a death.

Kudos to Andrea and Prudential for getting it right.

Adapt the Lessons To Your Situation

1. Do your people go out of their way to serve the customer, especially in sensitive situations?

Patience Shows Exemplary Service

I needed to have a document not only notarized, but "medallion-ized," which only the manager or assistant manager can do at my credit union. I called the manager to make sure he'd be there when I arrived and we set a time to meet.

I appeared at the appointed time only to learn he was at another branch! I didn't know he served two branches and he didn't mention where he'd be, thus the mix up. His assistant called him and he instructed me to see Elva, the assistant manager.

Elva was very helpful, but said she'd need to see a recent statement for the account, as she was attesting to the funds in the account. The manager hadn't asked for a statement for another account I'd had "medallion-ized" a few weeks earlier. I was the beneficiary of the account, not the account holder, so I was a bit miffed as it meant I'd need to get it and return.

I returned a few days later. This time, Elva read the documents more carefully. She discovered I also needed my father's death certificate, which of course I didn't have.

However, we wanted to verify this was really needed before I traipsed off once again.

So we called Franklin Templeton (where the account was held) and talked to the patient and courteous Stacy Base. Stacy confirmed that I did need the death certificate and helped us with some other details that were confusing. After assisting us in many areas, she connected us to a colleague who was an expert on other parts of our questions.

When I returned with the death certificate, Elva medallion-ized the document and I was done in moments.

I was impressed with not only Elva's patience in helping me through the confusion and offering to call Franklin Templeton, but her willingness to do some hand holding along the way.

Adapt the Lessons To Your Situation

1. If you are in two sites, do you communicate clearly where you'll meet your client?

2. Are your people willing to call a third party to help out a cutomer, or do they just tell the customer to call and get back to them?

3. Do your people help with a little handholding to help a customer in a confusing situation?

She was giving remark-abe service -- probably without even knowing it!

Door-to-Trunk Service

She was petite at 5'2", maybe weighing 115 lbs. As the door to her Park SFO off-airport bus opened so I could board, she rose from her driver's seat to stand in the doorway. She said hello with a big grin and reached out her hand to take my first bag.

I passed her my 3 bags then boarded myself. I noticed she did this for every passenger, although some of the bags looked to weigh nearly as much as she did. She greeted everyone with a friendly hello and never complained about their heavy luggage.

I was the last one to be left off at my car. I told her the nearest parking lot shed letter as well as my parking slot number. She drove right up to my car, opened the shuttle door and hopped out. She stood on the pavement as I passed down my luggage. She then raised the rolling handles and wheeled two of my pieces to my trunk.

Now that's remarkable service!

Adapt the Lessons To Your Situation

1. Do your staff perform their regular duties with a smile and friendly spirit?

2. Do they go out of their way to ease your customers' burden?

Waste Pick Up Mix Up

The landscape supply dump truck had piled my shredded redwood at the curb next to my driveway the day before my trash pick up. That same day, twenty-five feet away at the far end of my property, we piled the leaves and yard clippings for pick up by the yard-waste truck.

The driver got overzealous and scooped up the redwood as well as the yard waste. The previous week I had a shredded redwood pile in the same spot which he left, so who knows what prompted him to scoop it this time.

I was not a happy camper. I called the waste pickup company to see if anything could be done, knowing the answer could be "in our policy it says anything piled at the curb will be picked up," If so, I would have understood, but I was at least going to call.

I explained the situation to the receptionist. "Well, it was in the street where yard waste goes," she said unsympathetically. "I had another pile of shredded redwood there last week that he didn't touch. And it was 25 feet from the obvious yard waste of leaves and trimmings." She said to hold on, then that a supervisor would be over in a few minutes.

When I saw his pickup truck pull to my curb, I went

to the sidewalk to talk to him. He got out of his truck without saying anything nor making eye contact. He was fiddling with his cell phone ear piece so I thought he was on the phone. Yet he didn't say a word. He walked to the redwood pile remains, retracing the streaks of debris until he came to the yard waste remains. He talked into to his walkie-talkie to the pickup driver, asking him about the situation. Still no acknowledgement of me, verbally or visually.

When he was off his call, I explained the situation. He said he could see that the redwood was clearly in a different pile and his driver shouldn't have picked it up. He said the driver needed to pay more attention to what he's doing, since he'd been doing this job for years he should know better. He said he'd been doing some other things that showed he wasn't paying attention and he was now going to be suspended for a few days.

I told him the redwood had cost me $35 plus a $50 delivery fee. He called his boss and explained the situation. The boss agreed to reimburse me, but said he wasn't happy about it. We agreed I'd fax him the invoice from the landscape supply company after I had it replaced and he'd send me a check.

This is a mixed tale of some inappropriate customer-contact behavior but with an ending that took care of the customer.

1. The pickup driver was not paying attention, since it is common in my neighborhood to have land-scape materials dumped at your curb. I learned

that the drivers are instructed to not pick up something if there is doubt, but instead to leave a pre-prepared note at the house explaining the customer should call if they want the pile picked up.

2. The receptionist should have first tried to quell my frustration by empathizing, not negating my perspective.

3. The supervisor should have acknowledged me when he got out of the truck. If he was on the phone, he could have easily made eye contact, nodded and showed non-verbally that he was on the phone. When he was off the phone, he could have greeted me and found out the story.

On the positive side, the supervisor came within minutes of my call. He understood what happened and didn't doubt my story. He arranged for reimbursement and was pleasant about the situation.

Whenever there is a challenging situation, it's important to be especially aware of how you are interacting with the customer. From what you say to their explanation of the situation, to making sure you greet them verbally or non-verbally. Each piece of the interaction will enhance the customer's impression of your professionalism or detract from it.

Adapt the Lessons
To Your Situation

1. In your organization, how are you showing empathy (or not) when a customer explains a problem, even if you think the customer is wrong?

2. How do you acknowledge the presence of an in-person customer when you are on the phone?

Case Studies and Discussions of Customer Disservice

"Kindness and consideration are always in demand," but more so after horrific events.

What is Causing Your Upset Customers?

A recent issue of the consulting firm Yankelovich's newsletter, "Monitor," got me thinking again about the customer experience. The article was about civility and how "kindness and consideration are always in demand," but more so after horrific events. I believe people are looking for human connection in the face of tragedies that leave people thinking, "That's horrible. What if that were me or my family in trouble?"

However, we've seen human grace, patience and forgiveness fall to the wayside more frequently. From the person who cuts you off in traffic, to hassling the airline gate agent because a flight is delayed, to talking loudly on cell phones in restaurants, airports and other public places. Recently, in a sparsely populated restaurant, I couldn't help but overhear a woman's cell phone conversation loudly recounting her colonoscopy experience. Talk about an appetite depressant!

In 2003, Pew and Public Agenda released a study

titled "Aggravating Circumstances." It states, "Not only do eight in 10 Americans in our study say a lack of respect and courtesy is a serious problem, but six in 10 say things have become worse in recent years. A surprising 41 percent admit that they're part of the problem and sometimes behave badly themselves. More than a third (35 percent) admit to being aggressive drivers, at least occasionally, while 17 percent of those with cell phones admit to using them in a loud or annoying way.

"Americans say that disrespect, lack of consideration and rudeness are serious, pervasive problems that affect them on a personal, gut level. [They] say they are witnessing a deterioration of courtesy and respectfulness that has become a daily assault on their sensibilities and the quality of their lives."

But what does this have to do with your business?

The report continues: "[M]ost human enterprises proceed more smoothly if people are respectful and considerate of one another, and they easily become poisoned if people are unpleasant and rude." So all of your employees are affected by inconsiderate colleagues they must encounter. This cultivates resentfulness, bitterness, lack of motivation and low morale. Shoddy work ensues, and ultimately poor customer interactions.

On this topic, the report says, "Americans say that the way they are treated by business and customer service employees is frequently exasperating, and sometimes even insulting. Too many workers, they complain, are careless, apathetic and unhelpful."

With rude and discourteous behavior rising on both sides of the customer service counter, it's important that your people have the skills to not only avoid being disrespectful and discourteous themselves, but to disarm those customers who think this is the most effective way to get what they want.

Which is why my book Calming Upset Customers, *which first came out in 1989, is still a great seller. It is packed with ideas on how to avoid irritating your customers, then how to salve their pain if that fails. And how to manage your emotions afterward so you can treat the next customer professionally.*

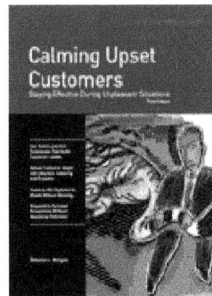

Calming Upset Customers

I'm happy to autograph any books ordered through my web site or on the phone. Just tell me to whom to autograph it when you order.

Adapt the Lessons To Your Situation

1. Have you noticed an increase in irritable customers?

2. When you encounter an irritated customer, how do you keep yourself from being surly?

Do Your Staff Head Off Customer Upsets?

I'd stayed at the Bejaya Time Square Hotel on my last visit to Kuala Lumpur a few months earlier. It's a nice business hotel attached to a very large mall. My previous room was a junior suite with a small kitchen area and living room, and Internet access via a DSL cable. I assumed I'd have a similar room this time.

My room was a tad smaller and not as well laid out. I immediately started my computer and saw no wireless signal. I tried plugging in my travel Ethernet cable, but it didn't fit in the wall slot. As he helped me with my bags, I asked the bellman if there was a DSL cable in the room. He said he'd be right back with one. I unpacked and got ready for an appointment with a business friend. The bellman didn't return.

Twenty minutes later, I called the front desk and was told they would send a cable right up. I said I was leaving in a few minutes, so just leave it in the room.

Ninety minutes later, I returned from my appointment to discover there was no cable awaiting. I called the front desk again. "We'll send one right up." Fifteen minutes later, no cable. I called again. "We'll bring one right up." I said, "This is the fourth time I've heard that and no one has arrived." As you guessed, twenty minutes passed and no cable.

I called again. I got a new person who said, "There is no Internet access from your room." "What???? Why didn't anyone tell me this before?" No clear reason, just "I'm sorry." When I said I must have access, as I was staying for five days, I was told I'd have to change rooms." I was already settled in and unpacked. What a pain!

I was livid. I went down to the front desk and asked to see the Manager on Duty (MOD). She saw a new key with my name on it. As I tried to explain the situation, she busily looked up my folio on the computer without looking at me. She said they would move me into a nicer room with Internet access and she'd waive the Internet fee." I was unhappy that 4 people told me they'd have a solution to my situation, and none of them delivered nor told me their solution wouldn't work. I'd waited 2.5 hours to be told the truth. Now I was having to move rooms, and I was exhausted from my long travel day.

When I asked the MOD why the front desk clerk hadn't informed me there was no Internet access in my room, she said, "Did you ask?" She was trying to blame this on me. I said, "I have stayed here before and there was no problem. This is a business hotel. Internet is a given. Should I have also had to ask if the room had a bed?"

She gave me my key. I packed and moved to the new room, and the Internet worked fine.

How could four people tell me they would solve my problem, then not only not deliver, but not know that their solution would not be an answer? Did they not know which rooms in the hotel had Internet access and which didn't? Wouldn't that have been an important piece of information to have before promising a solution that wouldn't work? They could have easily looked this up and called me back if they discovered my room was not enabled.

And then why would the MOD try to put the onus of the problem back on the customer, when the problem was one of a lack of a common room component?

This could have been easily avoided if the front desk clerk had been thinking. He noted that I was at the hotel for a business conference. Don't 98% of business guests, especially those from abroad, need Internet access? If so, shouldn't that be a standard question at check in, "Will you need Internet access?" If the response is, "I didn't bring a computer," then the clerk could say, "We have a business center if you find you need access." Or if the guest says, "Yes, I have my laptop," the clerk would then know to assign an Internet-enabled room.

What are your staff doing to head off upsets by thinking beyond rote transactions?

Adapt the Lessons To Your Situation

1. What did the service provider(s) do well?

2. What could the service provider(s) have done better?

3. What can you adapt from this story to implement in your organization?

Customs Officers Should Learn the Custom of Respect

heir job is to prevent any contraband from entering the US. But did these Customs officials have to be so darned surly in the process?

Some enforcement officers believe that they need to be human pit bulls and project an air that would have scofflaws cower. I beg to differ. I think one can be imposing while being respectful. These officials are the first impression many foreigners have of Americans on US turf. So why allow belittling behavior? Let me share examples from two Customs officers at Los Angeles International Airport on two occasions, a few months apart.

One gruff gray-haired officer barked at a foreigner who barely spoke English. There was a large "stop" sign a yard in front of the officer's station. This was intended to give each person a little privacy as the officer grilled his current victim. The elderly Chinese man did not stop at the sign but mistakenly stood behind his travel mate. The officer ordered, "Go back to the stop sign. How much bigger does it need to be?"

When it was my turn, he sternly demanded, "What took you out of the country?" Matching his militaristic tone, I replied, "I attended a conference." He continued his interrogation, "What business are you in?" "The seminar business." "What kind of seminars?" Looking him straight in the eye, I responded, "Customer service." (In retrospect my impish self wishes I'd said, "Teaching Customs officers to treat travelers with respect." But I probably would have been detained.) He softened a bit and waived me through.

The second officer had a similar demeanor. The middle-aged foreign woman in front of me seemed harried trying to keep her abundant luggage on the cart. When it was her turn, a bag fell off the cart and impeded her progress to the officer's stand. She struggled to put it back on the cart. He chastised her, "Come on lady, I don't have all day!"

I know that being a Customs officer, questioning thousands of people a day, can be grueling. I know that the people who are drawn to this kind of work can be into power as they can delay or deny entry into the country, or can confiscate bags, or even arrest someone if illegal substances are found. But I'd be surprised if they had even one arrest a day. So they are jerks to thousands of innocent people a day because of the premise that any of them could be a smuggler.

This is no way to welcome people to the US. Many policemen, for example, balance their role as enforcers with that of public relations. They know how to be firm but respectful. (I know there are bad apples in the police force, too.)

If your staff are in the position of enforcement, they need to learn how to do so while not being downright mean. There's no reason to do that when 99.9% of the people with whom they interact are law-abiding.

Adapt the Lessons To Your Situation

1. Have you ever been tempted to be brusk or short with a customer? What can cause that behavior?

2. What could the Customs officers have done better?

3. What can you adapt from this story to implement in your organization?

Do Your Staff Exemplify Your Advertisements' Promise of Superior Service?

ompanies can pay millions of dollars in advertising their superior service. But if their staff doesn't actually deliver that service, that advertising sets up expectations that aren't met, then get unhappy customers. I had first-hand experience with this mismatch.

I was excited about flying Emirates Air, as a friend waxed on about their service. Granted, he flew in one of their First Class suites (private bedroom, shower available). I was in coach. Although I'd flown Singapore Air a number of times, I wanted to check out the Emirates service to see how it compared. My 15-hour non-stop flight trip from SFO to Dubai got off to a rocky start at check in. The gate agent was insistent that my carry-on not exceed their 7 kg limit.

I took everything out of my Travel Pro bag (the kind flight crews carry) and empty it weighed 5 kg. My laptop weighed another 3. I was already over the weight limit and I didn't even have my purse, jewelry or on-flight reading in the bag. I told him I wasn't comfortable checking my jewelry and he didn't allow an exception. So I quickly stuffed my jewelry boxes into the outside zipper compartment of my checked bag, as he wouldn't allow me to board with an overweight bag.

Big mistake.

When I unpacked in my room in Dubai, the outside zipper was partly undone and the case for a pearl necklace and earrings was gone. I felt stupid for

1) checking the jewelry in the first place when in the light of hindsight it would have been smarter to just wear it or put it in my pocket; and

2) not taking the time to unlock my bag and put it in the locked compartment.

The agents in Dubai were little help. When I tried to explain what happened they kept thinking I lost the jewelry from my carry-on bag. They said I should have reported it before I left the Dubai airport. How could I, when I didn't know it was missing until I unpacked?

I decided the best way to handle it would be in person at the airport. The agents there were of no help either. I thought, "How hard can this be? It either fell out in SFO or in Dubai. Don't they have a luggage lost and found?" Evidently, no.

When I brought this up with the supervisor at the gate she, too, didn't seem to understand. I asked politely for her supervisor. None came. She said to check at SFO. But she did upgrade me to business class!

Business class was great — lie-flat seats, an extra 1-inch mattress to make it more comfortable, in-seat massage units, larger video screens, better amenities and food. The 15 hours passed quickly.

At SFO I went immediately to baggage claim to ask about lost and found. While pleasant, they said I had to call LA to report the loss. Again, couldn't they just check lost and found? Evidently this was impossible. I took the names and phone numbers of the men "helping" me and gave them mine. I asked them if they would check lost and found and call me in the next two days, no matter what they discovered. They agreed.

I called the LA number the next business day and left a message with the pertinent info. I waited a week. No return call and nothing from the men in SFO who promised to call whether they found something or not. I called the LA number again and got a public affairs man. We talked for 20 minutes. He, too, didn't listen, thinking I lost something on board even though I clearly explained I was forced to put my jewelry in the checked bag at check in.

He informed me that jewelry is not covered as stated in their rules of carriage. Since I did not intend to pack my pearl necklace and earrings, I didn't review their policy that states they don't cover jewelry. However, I'd have appreciated the agent refreshing my memory as he saw me pack my jewelry in the checked bag.

He also said they didn't cover pilferage. I said, "You hire people who steal?" He said it happens, and if someone is caught they are fired and punished. He said he'd send me a form to complete.

It is a month later and I have yet to receive their form, let alone an apology.

I am grateful for the Dubai agent who did not have to upgrade me. It does not replace my pearls, but it was a nice treat.

However, the lack of anyone taking any ownership of my issue, including not following through with promised phone calls or mailing me complaint documents, is their problem.

Am I overly picky because I'm an expert on customer complaint management? Perhaps. But actually, I'm always looking for great examples to include in my seminars. Unfortunately, this example will be on the thumbs down side when I wish it had been thumbs up.

Will I fly Emirates again? If I am going to Dubai, yes, as the non-stop from SFO saves me 10 hours over any other airline. Will I come better prepared with lighter carry ons? Absolutely! Do I hate Emirates? No. Do I love them? Not as much as Singapore Airlines, but way better than most US carriers when flying internationally.

Adapt the Lessons To Your Situation

1. What did the service provider(s) do well?

2. What could the service provider(s) have done better?

3. What can you adapt from this story to implement in your organization?

Does your staff help your customers save time, money and aggravation, rather than causing more of these?

Do Your Staff Understand the Customer Experience?

Are your staff putting themselves in your customers' shoes, thinking through the customer experience? Does your staff help your customers save time, money and aggravation, rather than causing more of these?

Twice recently, with two different reps at my travel agency, I found they didn't really understand the customer experience, so I ended up spending more time, money and hassle than necessary.

Both were when I was traveling internationally from LAX. The first rep told me I could not fly out of my local airport, San Jose, which is a 10-15 minute, $20 cab ride. Instead she said I had to fly out of San Francisco, an hour's drive and $125 cab ride. I told her I thought it odd that I couldn't catch the flight to LAX from SJC, but she said no, I had to go out of SFO.

Planning a second trip, I called when the rep was out of the office and the agency owner took my call. I asked if he knew why I couldn't fly out of SJC. He said I could. Tap, tap, tap — a few keystrokes later the flight was booked — saving me 1.5 hours and $210.

The rep also booked me on a SJC/LAX flight which would have me arrive 5 hours before my connection. When I pushed back that I didn't want to sit in LAX that long, she gave me another option arriving 2 hours before my international departure. If I hadn't said anything, I would be cooling my heels at LAX for an extra 3 hours.

The next rep booked me from LAX to SJC on Southwest. While I normally don't mind flying Southwest, after an 24-hour travel day, the last thing I wanted was to claim my luggage and schlep it half-way the length of the airport to stand in line at Southwest to check it again. Other domestic carriers transfer baggage inner-line, but Southwest won't. The rep didn't understand how exhausting it is to fly for nearly 24 hours, then have this unnecessary hassle. There are multiple flights hourly from LAX to SJC that she could have chosen. But she didn't inform me of the SW baggage issue; she just booked it.

Your customer contact staff need to have familiarity with your product or service from the customer's perspective. They need to either use the product regularly or visit a customer site and watch the customer use it, as well as talk to those who use it, not just Purchasing. If they can't put themselves in the end-user's position, it is harder for them to suggest solutions that will best serve the customer. And we know customers who feel their needs are understood are very likely to keep buying from you.

Adapt the Lessons
To Your Situation

1. What did the service provider(s) do well?

2. What could the service provider(s) have done better?

3. What can you adapt from this story to implement in your organization?

He threw them back into the box.

How Do Your People React to Dissatisfied Customers?

I was returning the $200 Z-Coil sports shoes I thought would help my heel pain. I'd purchased them the previous week with the provision I could return them with no restocking fee if my physical therapist didn't approve of how they supported my feet. It took me a few days longer to get in to see her than I thought.

Andrew, the manager, said I could wear them around my house to see how they felt and still return them if needed. I did just that.

My PT said the coil in the heel was too unstable for me. I explained this to the salesman at the counter when I retuned the shoes. He said he would refund me minus a "sanitation" fee. I told him Andrew, who was helping another customer, said there was no return fee. Andrew came to the counter and looked at the shoes. He threw them back into the box and said they were too worn to waive the fee. I told him I wore them only around the house, as we had agreed. He gave me a disgusted look.

I was not surly or belligerent. I was calm, yet clear on what we had agreed. There was no need for him to throw the shoes in the box nor give me the look he did.

As a result, I will never recommend anyone to this store, and on their feedback form I pointed out Andrew's lack of professionalism. Other customers in the store heard the interaction.

How could Andrew have handled it differently?

He could have said, "I'm sorry these didn't work out for you. I thought they would. I realize I said there would be no return fee when you thought you'd see your PT the next day, so there would only have been a day of wear around the house. You've had these shoes a week and it appears they've been worn longer than I expected, thus the need for them to be sanitized for the next customer. I hope you understand we want the shoes to be fresh for whomever owns them next."

If he looked me in the eye while sharing this and behaved maturely and respectfully, I would have had no ill feelings. The sad part is that his behavior cost him my referrals for others who have foot problems, as these shoes were touted by a friend with the same malady. They just didn't work for my needs.

How are your people behaving when a customer returns an item? Are they treating the customer respectfully or not? If not, are other customers within earshot, watching, listening and thinking, "Is this how I'll be treated if I have a problem with my purchase?" Probably.

Every business has unhappy customers. How they are treated will determine if they will get surly, return for future purchases, or refer others. It's not hard to treat a customer well. But if your people aren't trained and monitored they can behave like Andrew and not only lose a customer, but referrals as well as perhaps customers within earshot who are considering a purchase.

Adapt the Lessons To Your Situation

1. How do you treat customers who want to return a purchase?

2. How do you ensure you don't react like Andrew?

3. What can you adapt from this story to implement in your organization?

The Less-Than-Festive Holiday Lunch Service

A friend and I scheduled a special holiday lunch at one of the finest San Francisco hotels. Unfortunately, the service we received was less than we'd get at a take-out restaurant. Let me share the story and then examine what could have been done.

▲ We arrived at our reservation time and there were two parties ahead of us in line, neither with reservations. We waited over 10 minutes for them to be seated in the half-full restaurant before we could even state that we had a reservations.

Wouldn't it be grand if there were two lines at restaurants, one for folks checking in with reservations and one for those without. Shouldn't those who had the foresight and took the time to make reservations be given priority service?

▲ We waited 10 more minutes for our server to arrive. We gave her both our drink and lunch order, stating that we had already waited a while. She was apologetic and said they were short handed today. We smiled and nodded.

The customer doesn't really care why they are getting bad service. They should still get adequate service, even if it is not the best the establishment provides with a full staff.

▲ The meal came promptly and was delicious. I found a piece of metal in mine, like from a Christmas ornament. I put it aside, and since it wasn't disgusting, ate around where it had been and watched carefully to make sure there weren't more. I was engrossed in the conversation with my friend, so decided to point out the metal when the server returned. She didn't.

No foreign object should ever be in food, but usually the server checks back within minutes of the dishes being served to make sure everything is to the customers' liking. We didn't see our server again until we were finished.

▲ When she finally arrived to clear the plates, I gave her the metal and said she should show the chef. She apologized and said she'd show the manager immediately. "Why didn't you tell me?" she demanded. "Because you didn't ever check in with us." "You should have waived me over," she countered. I wanted to say, "I was focused on my friend, not on tracking you down." But I didn't.

Service staff should never make the customer wrong

for the server not doing their job.

⚠ She left and told the manager about my find. She was back within minutes to say they were comping our meal and would like to comp dessert and coffee if we'd like. We took her up on the offer and thanked her politely.

They did as they should have — comped my meal. It was generous of the manager to comp my friend's too, as well as dessert.

This is a grand old hotel, with a beautifully appointed dining room. Too bad our experience of their service was way below par.

Have you audited your customer service lately? How do your staff respond when something is wrong with a meal? Do they make the customer wrong?

Adapt the Lessons To Your Situation

1. What did the server do well?

2. What could the server have done better?

3. What can you adapt from this story to implement in your organization?

Do You Know How Your Customers Are Being Treated?

M eeting with a potential client for a customer service improvement project, I asked if they monitored their staff's phone calls. The response was what I hear from 95% of my clients.

"No."

When I asked why not, there was some stumbling and fumbling and the bottom line was they hadn't thought of it.

If you aren't periodically monitoring your people's customer service calls, here's a compelling story for why you should.

A *Des Moines Register* article recently revealed that Nationwide Mutual Insurance fired five customer service reps who routinely hung up on policyholders trying to file claims after fires, traffic accidents or other events covered by their insurance policies.

One of the workers was found to have hung up on 34 percent of her callers. Another hung up on 8 percent of callers; one hung up on about 50 policyholders over a two-week period.

Why did these reps do this?

▲ **Feeling put upon.** One felt justified in routinely hanging up on policyholders other company representatives transferred to her. "I didn't think it was fair that they could keep transferring all of their work over to us," she stated. "So when I would see on the phone that it was a transfer from them, I would just hang up."

▲ **Bump job stats.** Another hung up to boost her job-performance statistics.

▲ **Selfish thinking.** "I didn't think about the fact that it could be someone that was needing help right then and there, that their daughter may have just got in an accident and was in the hospital and they were needing help. I wasn't really thinking about the customer. I was thinking about myself and my stats."

How could this happen?

▲ **Little accountability.** Although the Nationwide spokeswoman said the company regularly monitors workers' performance, obviously not enough.

▲ **Measuring the wrong things.** Reps reported they hung up to increase their job stats. So number of calls taken and average talk time were probably part of what they monitored. It appears no one had the job of listening in periodically to the calls to see what was happening. Which would be especially important if you saw a lot of the talk times were in seconds. You'd scratch your head and wonder why that was. Then you'd listen in and hear "click, click, click." You'd then know something was amiss.

⚠ **No feedback.** If you don't know that your folks are doing anything wrong, how can you coach them? You can't. Someone was asleep at the wheel.

⚠ **Hiring the wrong people.** Part of the hiring process is ensuring you get people who care about other people. That's also why you have a probationary period. While someone can be on their best behavior in an interview and for a few months, their true nature often comes out before the end of the sixth month. I'm betting these reps showed their true colors before they became permanent employees. Or if they were transferred from within the company, best to monitor them as if they are a new employee. And one would think that with these attitudes, they'd be complaining to others. Where were their supervisors to hear their comments and step up their supervision?

The question for you: Are you paying close enough attention to how your customers are being treated? If not, why not? Excuses like, "We'd get complaints if they did that," or "We don't have enough time to monitor," or "We trust our reps." These make sense on the surface. And I bet Nationwide said them all at one time.

Adapt the Lessons To Your Situation

1. What's the value of regularly monitoring ever customer service provider's performance?

2. How could you increase your monitoring, or asking to be monitored if you are the service provider?

3. What can you adapt from this story to implement in your organization?

There Ought to be a Law — Customer Disservice

In the last week, I've encountered three situations that have totally ignored the customer having a positive experience. Each one is an example of someone just doing what they have been told, without any thinking through of the implications for the customer.

▲ While waiting to board a commuter plane, the agent announced all passengers should exit the gate and wait on the tarmac. So 50 of us were herded out in 90-degree weather to be buffeted by the jet spray of our incoming plane, wait for the passengers to deplane, watch the pilots do their pre-fight check and the ground personnel clean the plane. After 20 minutes in the hot sun, we were then allowed to cross the steaming tarmac to board.

Why couldn't we have sat comfortably in the air-conditioned waiting room while the plane landed, passengers disembarked, and the plane was checked and cleaned? It would have been a lot more comfortable, and we could have had another 20 minutes of productive time working or reading.

▲ I received a letter regarding my AmEx merchant account telling me one of my customers had reported fraudulent charges on her account. Her charge to us would be deducted from my account unless I could dig up proof of her purchase and fax it back to them. However, they included a list of every charge on her bill during the challenged time and she had to mark "I take responsibility for this charge" or "This is a fraudulent charge" on each item. She had marked the charge for my item as the former. Yet I had to prove the charge or I would be docked the payment.

Why should I have to waste my time proving something she takes responsibility for? After calling AmEx they said there was no way around this. Is this stupid, or what?

▲ I arrived as instructed at 11:15 for my 11:30 doctor appointment. The pre-exam paperwork took less than one minute, but that is the reason they asked me to appear early. At 11:45 I was called by the medical assistant to take blood pressure, temperature and weight. I was shown to the exam room, told to disrobe and put on those skimpy paper covers. At 12:15 the doctor appeared.

Why should a patient be kept waiting for 30 minutes essentially naked? Couldn't the MA take the vitals, then put the patient in the exam room, but told not to get undressed until closer to when the doctor is ready? I know doctors have tight schedules and can't wait for patients to undress, but couldn't she let the MA know when she was finishing up with the previous patient so the new patient can be informed to disrobe now?

All of these examples are of procedures designed for the company, not for the customer. As people get fed up with being treated like cattle, they will take their business elsewhere, to those who show some modicum of care about the customer experience.

Adapt the Lessons To Your Situation

1. When was the last time you aske your customers about their experience with your organization and asked for ideas for improvements in your processes?

2. How could you improve your customer's experience of doing business with you?

3. What can you adapt from this story to implement in your organization?

Are Your Staff Resourceful?

I had flown in to deliver the keynote speech for a customer service conference at a resort. Because of weather delays and too-tight connections, I hadn't eaten since lunch, and now, after 9:00 p.m., the destination airport concessions were closed. I asked my driver to stop at a fast food place so I could eat during our hour-long drive, but he said there weren't any on our route but he could go 30 minutes out of our way to find one. I opted to wait until I arrived at the beach resort, assuming since it was a well-known mid-range chain there would be at least room service.

At 10:15, when checking in, I asked if the restaurant was still open. "No," came the reply from the front desk clerk. "How about room service?" I hopefully asked. "No, they close at 10:00, too." Can you call the restaurant manager, as he might still be there?" "He's gone home."

My overtired brain continued asking about options. "Is there a mini-bar in my room?" "No." "Vending machines?" "No." She was not picking up on my hunger cues. I went to my room and called room service myself, just to check. No one answered.

Luckily, I had my travel almond stash to stave off the hunger. But I was hungry for more than food — I was starved for resourcefulness!

In a comparable situation for your staff, how resourceful would they be? Would they think beyond the obvious? Would they stick with it until a solution was found?

The next day I told this story from the platform to illustrate how staff behaves when no management is around to observe. The hotel sales rep responsible for my group caught wind of my plight and apologized. She said, "There were other options she should have known to offer. The bar has free popcorn, so even though it was closed, she could have had the manager on duty open it to get some for you."

When I said I was just looking for something to stop my stomach's rumblings, popcorn, or a little cheese and crackers and a banana would have been fine.

She said, "The manager on duty could have opened the kitchen for you and easily done crackers, cheese and fruit for you. It would have taken 5 minutes." But calling the manager on duty was not offered nor done.

She went on, "Or she could have told you about the pizza delivery options, or Waiters on Wheels — the menus are at the front desk. Or the nearby 7-11 or a 24-hour fast food place a 5-minute cab drive away." None were suggested.

So instead of just leaving a famished traveler to her

own devices — and almonds — this hotel has now given me a story to illustrate how unresourceful your staff may be and you'll never know. But now several hundred people know — and they know the hotel's name and location.

How are your people doing in the resourcefulness department? Have someone check. Or you'll never know.

Adapt the Lessons
To Your Situation

1. How resourceful are the people on your team?

2. With others on your team, brainstorm some customer situations and come up with a list of optons.

3. What can you adapt from this story to implement in your organization?

Are You Doing Stupid Things to Your Customers?

Flying back from a speaking engagement in Ann Arbor last week, I changed planes in Chicago. I boarded the American Eagle flight at the appointed time. We sat at the gate for nearly half an hour after departure time when the co-pilot came on the intercom.

"Ladies and gentleman, the reason we haven't taken off is we have no pilot. Our pilot called in sick and we've notified an on-call pilot. We expect him to be here shortly."

Half an hour later, we are told the pilot had arrived and we'll be taking off soon.

So what's wrong with this picture? Crew must report in at least a half hour before departure time. So flight management knew there was no pilot at minimum 30 minutes beforehand, even if the scheduled pilot hadn't called in. So why would they board us all, and let us sit like sardines in a little plane with no food, drink or Internet access for 30 minutes when we could have been more comfortable in the waiting area?

It couldn't have to do with on-time departure ratings, as they knew we couldn't push back without a pilot. So what were they thinking? That this was a good way to treat their customers? How could anyone possibly think this was a good idea?

With JetBlue's Customer Bill of Rights policy, we would have had to sit there over an hour before getting any compensation. I think sitting in a crammed plane at a gate is close to cruel and unusual punishment, and I was only stuck for an hour. I can't imagine how those passengers on JetBlue lasted 11 hours. I would have chewed my way out the emergency exit.

Are you doing stupid things to your customers without thinking? Once someone saw it was going to be an hour before takeoff, couldn't they have seen the folly of our boarding and invited us to deplane for that hour?

Are you empowering your people to think through what the customer is experiencing and make on-the-spot decisions to help ease their discomfort? Are you rewarding behavior that shows your people are thinking of creating a positive customer experience instead of a negative one?

Consider eliciting examples for stupid customer service behaviors so others can learn what happened and discuss alternatives if the situation presents itself again. If you hide the mistakes, no one will learn how to avoid them in the future.

Adapt the Lessons To Your Situation

1. What have you learned lately from mistakes your organization has made with customers?

2. Have you examined your customer procedures and policies lately and suggested changing ones that aren't very customer friendly?

3. What can you adapt from this story to implement in your organization?

When they get a question outside the norm, they just seem to shut off their brain, resulting in either no sales where there could have been one, or elongating the buying process if they could just think.

Can Your Staff Think?

O ften times I find the staff of businesses don't know how to think beyond pre-described processes. When they get a question outside the norm, they just seem to shut off their brain, resulting in either no sales where there could have been one, or elongating the buying process if they could just think.

At OfficeMax I found an item on the clearance rack that I wanted. I proceeded to the checkout counter knowing it wasn't priced, so I asked the cashier.

"This was in the clearance area but there's no price. Can you tell me the clearance price?"

"Sure. Let me scan it. The scan says 1 cent so that means I can't sell it."

"Well, it's on the clearance rack and I'd like to buy it."

"But the register isn't giving me a price."

"Well, the item is clearly for sale."

"When it comes up as 1 cent it means it should be destroyed."

"Well, it is in good shape and I'd buy it if I could get a price. Could the manager help?"

"I'll call him over."

He came over, I explained the situation, he came up with a price. How hard was that?

Why did it take my prodding the cashier to get her to see the illogic of her argument. Here is an item on the clearance table in good shape, but because her system brings up a "must destroy" price she can't sell it to a willing customer? If that was too much for her to think through, couldn't she immediately think to call in her manager?

Are you making it difficult for your customers to buy what they want to buy because your systems and non-thinking employees are preventing customers from parting with their money?

I encourage you to aggressively eavesdrop on your front-line employees to see if they are thinking or just reciting "policy" drivel — even when it makes no sense for the situation.

Adapt the Lessons To Your Situation

1. What is your procedure for when a front-line employee doesn't know the answer to a customer's question?

2. What can you adapt from this story to implement in your organization?

*How do your non-front line
employees interactions
influence your customers?*

What Are Your Non-"Front Line" People Saying to Your Customers?

Have you thought about how employees who aren't your usual "customer service providers" in your company affect your customers? These are the people who don't get customer service training because they don't often interact with customers. They could be in accounting, maintenance, production, or information services. Or shuttle services.

When they do interact with customers, what are they saying? How does their interaction influence your customers? Here's an example.

I was taking a shuttle to pick up my rental car. I overheard the driver sharing a story with another customer.

"See that rabbit? There are lots of rabbits in these fields. Last week one ran in front of the bus, and I didn't have time to swerve. I ran right over him. We heard a tha-thump as he went under my wheels.

"Well, there's this little kid sitting here in the front with his mom. He sees the rabbit, then hears the tha-thump. He says, 'What was that?' I said, 'I guess it was the Easter Bunny.' He starts bawling! Some kids can't take a joke."

Imagine yourself as this little boy's mom. How do you feel about this representative of the car rental company? How, then, do you feel about the company? Are you likely to go out of your way to rent from this company again?

Imagine yourself sitting with me on the shuttle when I heard the story. How do you feel about this driver's sensitivity? Do you, at some level, worry that this attitude is shared by his co-workers? Do you wonder what kind of management would hire and not coach someone with this kind of inappropriate behavior? Are you on guard when you approach the next employee at the rental counter?

This may have been an isolated incident by one employee. However, many of us generalize this behavior. We might feel that not only did this employee have bad judgment about his comment to the little boy, but he may have bad judgment about other things as well. We may imagine his behavior is indicative of others in the company who share this kind of insensitivity. It may color how we perceive actions by other employees too. We may look for other indiscretions to prove our perceptions right. And if we find them, we may decide not to rent from this company again.

The bottom line is: even non-"front line" employees need to be trained and coached to ensure that everyone is responding appropriately any time they interact with customers. We never know who may be listening.

Adapt the Lessons To Your Situation

1. How are your non-front line employees trained, monitored and coached?

2. What can you adapt from this story to implement in your organization?

The Copy Catastrophe

W hile out of town for a client, I enter the national copy shop chain to pick up a large order I'd left the day before. An employee, Bill, helps me.

RM: I have an order to pick up. It's under Morgan.

Bill: Ah, yes. I spoke to you this morning when you called. Here it is. It's a big order.

RM: I want to verify that I was charged 95¢ for the binding, rather than $1.95. I got a break because of quantity.

Bill: I'll check it when the receipt comes out of the register. Hmm. The computer keeps spinning when I enter your customer number.

RM: I gave my customer number to Trina yesterday so you could download my information from corporate.

Bill: Let me see if Mike can help. (He confers with Mike, who suggests he open another register. By this time there are about 20 people in the store, many of whom are waiting for assistance.) It will take a minute for this register to boot up.

Bill goes to help other customers. About 10 minutes pass. He returns to the original register to see that my order has come up.

Bill: Your order has come up now.

RM: Would it help if you used my corporate charge card?

Bill: Let me see. (He stares at the screen, not seeming to know what to do with my card.)

RM: The other stores just swipe it like a credit card.

Mike punches something on the screen so Bill can now swipe my card.

Bill: Now I just have to find you in our customer list.

He fiddles around for a few minutes. He tries to get Mike to help, but it takes a while for Mike to respond.

Bill to Mike: I can't find her account. It's not listed in alphabetical order.

Mike to Bill: Just do a account name search. Here, help my customer. (They switch roles.)

After another few minutes, Mike prints out my receipt. There are 5 people waiting behind me to be rung out, and another 10 in Bill's line for help.

RM: (looking over the bill) I want to verify that I was only charged 95¢ for the binding. It says $1.95 here, unless you can show me where that was reversed.

Mike: I wish you'd told me that before I rung you out.

RM (working to control the anger): *I did tell Bill that at the beginning of this transaction.*

Mike needn't have made that last comment. He could have acknowledged that I'd been waiting 20 minutes to do a simple transaction. He made an already bad situation worse. I'd been pleasant, helpful, and patient up to that point.

Epilogue

A few days later I had to return for some more copies. This time the manager, Stan, assisted me. I couldn't help tell him this story, as I thought it would help him to coach his staff. He was empathic and apologetic.

Stan refigured my bill to make sure I had been charged the right amount, and found some errors. He credited my bill $40 of overcharges (more than 10% of my total), as well as comping my small order for that day. He thanked me for bringing it to his attention, as now he would bring up not only the way the first situation was handled, but how to figure up large orders.

How are your people dealing with customers in challenging situations? What are you doing to coach them when they haven't done it the way you'd like? And what are you doing to show the customer you not only appreciate his business, but that he brought it to your attention?

Adapt the Lessons To Your Situation

1. What did the service provider(s) do well?

2. What could the service provider(s) have done better?

3. What can you adapt from this story to implement in your organization?

Restaurant Service
Goes Blop!

A national restaurant chain has been running a series of coupons to lure customers to their restaurants. Unfortunately, once they've accomplished that, they don't create an experience that has customers wanting to come back. Here's my recent experience.

I arrived at 5:30 to have a quick bite to eat. I had two coupons, one for $10 off of a $20 ticket and one for a free dessert for my birthday. I asked the server if I could combine them, and she said no, I had to choose. No problem.

She had only two other tables to serve. One with a family of 3 who ordered shortly after I was seated. Another table of 2 was awaiting another couple to join them so ordered just drinks.

She took my drink order, then my meal order when she brought the drink. I had a salad and pasta, two simple, quick-to-prepare options. The salad took 20 minutes to arrive, the pasta 20 minutes later. She walked by several times attending to the other tables, but never made eye contact nor stopped to see if I needed anything. When I'd eaten my fill, I waited for her to come by then asked for my bill, expaining I needed to go. And I asked for a take-home container.

She took my leftovers and returned 10 minutes later with the bill. If she'd brought the bill, then took the leftovers, the credit card could be processing while she boxed up the leftovers. She cleared my place of all utinsils and plates. When she brought the bill, she also brought a complimentary piece of cake, which she didn't have to do as I was using the $10 coupon. I thanked her, but said I'd need to have a take-home container since I had to go. She brought back a styrofoam container. But I had no utinsils to transfer the cake.

It took 35 mintues from when I asked for the bill to when I got out of there. I asked to see the manager but got tired of waiting, so left my card saying I'd like to speak to him. He never called.

While I realize servers have no control over how quickly the kitchen gets out the dishes, they do have control over how they manage their customers' experience. An occasional, "how are you doing?" or "Your pasta will be right out," or "How is your meal?" goes a long way. Then it would be nice to listen when your customer says they need to go and thinking of the most expedient way to help them go. Then is it too much to ask that the server be present to the fact that they have brought food after the customer has said they are full, and after you've cleared all the silverware? I spend 90 minutes having a dinner that should have taken 45.

Adapt the Lessons
To Your Situation

1. What did the server do well?

2. What could the server have done better?

3. What can you adapt from this story to implement in your organization?

I scratched my head about how the designers could be so clueless about customer service and convenience

Are Your Processes Designed for Your Staff's Convenience or Your Customers'?

love my library. It's steps away from me, just across an adjacent street. I order books online, then pop over and pick them up. So convenient.

But not everything in this newly rebuilt library is convenient — at least not for its patrons. There's a problem where staff convenience won out over patron service.

I take responsibility for not making sure this type of thing would not happen when the new library was designed. They held community meetings to hear what patrons wanted, and in the designers' defense, they incorporated many cool, state-of-the art features.

Which makes this one decision a glaring one to me. How could this oversight happen with so many community members attending the design meetings?

What's the problem I find so egregious?

The book return slot is at the back of the building and requires one to either walk down a narrow driveway or get out of their car to return books. Not that I'm endorsing laziness, but previously there was a drive-by drop bin (like a curbside postal box) that made it easy to return books. My library is on a busy street, so it would have made even more sense to put a book drop-off box on the street in a white-curbed zone so people could just pull over and drop off their books.

But now pedestrians have to go through the library and out the other side to drop off books in the designated slot. If the library is closed, they have to walk down the narrow driveway to the drop-off slot, sharing the driveway with any cars doing the same.

I scratched my head about how the designers could be so clueless about customer service and convenience, so I finally asked the head librarian. "Help me understand the logic in having the drop-off slot at the back and without the car drop off capability? What am I missing?"

He shook his head and nodded. "This is asked a lot. It is for the library staff's convenience. They don't have to go out in the weather to retrieve the books as they did when we had the drive through drop box."

Ah, so the staff doesn't have to go out and roll in a cart twice a day, hundreds of patrons a week are inconvenienced? Does this make sense? It's not as if the weather is torturous — it's Northern California for goodness sake! The weather is moderate. The book bins are on wheels so it doesn't take a lot of brawn to move them.

Adapt the Lessons
To Your Situation

1. Are your processes for the convenience of your staff or your customer?

2. If for your staff, can you reengineer the process so it is works for both parties?

3. Have you asked your customers how you can make all aspects of doing business with you easier? If so, do you take action on what they say?

4. When was the last time you looked at your processes from the customer experience perspective?

She replied, "Bruce is a temp. He can't make those promises."

Do You Honor What Your Employees Promise?

ike millions of other homeowners, I recently applied to refinance my mortgage at a lower rate. When a very low rate was advertised on my financial institution's web site, I acted so I could lock in the rate.

Wednesday morning I began to complete the convenient online application. At one point the curser spun and spun. The site said it was processing and if I got tired of waiting to click a button and someone from would contact me. After 10 minutes I clicked.

Thursday when no one contacted me I went back on the site and picked up where I left off. When I reached that page, the curser spun. I called and left a message for one of the loan offers I'd dealt with before. Later that day she emailed me that a different loan officer would be in contact that day.

The next day with no contact, I called again. Neither loan officer I knew was available so I was asked if I'd like to speak to someone else in the department. Sure. I talked to Bruce and explained the spinning curser and my concern about wanting to lock in the rate since it had now been 3 days. He said, "No problem. I'll figure out what's wrong with the web page and make sure you get the rate on the day you started this, as rates change on the weekend."

Monday late afternoon, one of the loan officers called. She looked at the online application and found a minor error that I would have never found. She corrected it and the spinning curser disappeared and I could proceed. I mentioned locking in the low rate from last week, as this week's rate was considerably higher. She said, "You can't lock in last week's rate since you didn't complete the application until today."

I was livid.

"I didn't complete the application because your system wouldn't let me. I called your colleague Thurs. and she said you'd call me back that day. When you didn't, I called Friday and got Bruce. He said he'd lock in the rate for me."

She replied, "Bruce is a temp. He can't make those promises."

I was even more livid.

"Bruce is a representative of your company so you have to honor his promises. How would I know he was a temp? Am I supposed to ask everyone with whom I interact if they are an employee or temp in order to know whether to believe what they tell me? That's not a way to do business."

She said she'd see what she could do.

When I didn't hear from her for another week, I called the department head explaining the scenario. At first he didn't want to honor the lower rate either, but eventually he gave in as my 20-year payment record with them is unblemished and I have a high credit score.

Adapt the Lessons To Your Situation

1. Are you holding your customers accountable to pay more because your systems are not functioning?

2. Are you not honoring what your employees promise your customers?

3. Are your employees clear on what they can and can't promise?

Housekeeping Asleep
at the Wheel

The upscale Houston hotel had just opened two weeks earlier. The hotel was appointed with trendy, hip furniture throughout. My corner room was no different. But just because it looked good, didn't mean the staff was up to par.

As I unpacked I opened a drawer to put away my belongings, I was surprised to see half a dozen pairs of men's socks and briefs. Luckily — they appeared clean! I've traveled a great deal in my 3 decades in business, but never found another's clothing in a hotel drawer.

Then I began putting my things in the bathroom. I noticed half-used open shampoo, rinse and soup in the shower. I began to wonder if the housekeeper had actually cleaned the room, although there were fresh amenities in the bathroom. I found other housekeeping-related issues — light bulbs burned out, mini-bar door broken, etc.

I can understand how a housekeeper could miss a burnt out light bulb, but there were just too many things to go unreported. I called and talked to the manager on duty. I felt he should know that the hotel had some week spots — specifically housekeeping — that were not congruent with the hotel's desire to be considered a high-end property.

I'm guessing the housekeeper meant well. Maybe she was new or distracted or not well trained. But each room has to be checked by an inspector. So where was s/he? Are your managers checking the staff's work, at least periodically, to make sure the quality standard is present?

Adapt the Lessons To Your Situation

1. Are you aware of where certain departments don't support the image your company wants?

2. Are there people who are asleep at the wheel that are undermining your image and/or brand?

Resources

Resources

o to www.RebeccaMorgan.com to access a variety of useful resources.

Customer service and management articles

We have over 200 pages of useful articles designed to help you manage your situations better.

Managers Discussion Guide Program

This program enables you to make your staff meetings come alive in 20-30 minutes per month, with no prep by you!

Books, MP3s and learning tools

High-quality tools to help you work more effectively.

Blog

Read new ideas and stories to grow your key talent.

Ezine

Subscribe to your free copy of *Insights and Information*, our periodic ezine full of tips and new ideas.